MAREK HORN

Marek Horn's debut play, *Wild Swimming*, premiered at the 2019 Edinburgh Festival Fringe and later enjoyed a sell-out run at Bristol Old Vic. A radio version was made for BBC Radio 4, and he is adapting it for the screen. He is working on further televisions projects of his own and has written on Happy Prince's upcoming adaptation of Jilly Cooper's beloved novel, *Rivals*, for Disney+. His play *Yellowfin* was produced at Southwark Playhouse in 2021.

He has been writer on attachment at Bristol Old Vic, the National Theatre Studio, and the RSC. He is a Creator in Residence at BBC Studios and in 2023 was the recipient of a Peggy Ramsay and Film4 Playwrights' Scheme Bursary, in conjunction with Hampstead Theatre.

T0352667

Other Titles in This Series

Marek Horn

OCTOPOLIS

NICK HERN BOOKS

London

www.nickhernbooks.co.uk

A Nick Hern Book

Octopolis first published in Great Britain as a paperback original in 2023 by Nick Hern Books Limited, The Glasshouse, 49a Goldhawk Road, London W12 8QP

Octopolis copyright © 2023 Marek Horn

Marek Horn has asserted his right to be identified as the author of this work

Cover image by rawpixel.com on Freepik

Designed and typeset by Nick Hern Books, London
Printed in Great Britain by Mimeo Ltd, Huntingdon, Cambridgeshire PE29 6XX

A CIP catalogue record for this book is available from the British Library

ISBN 978 1 83904 262 1

www.nickhernbooks.co.uk/environmental-policy

For Rebecca

My other self
My remaining limbs

The formal definition of human nature preferred by patriarchal culture is one based on the articulation of sound. As Aristotle says, any animal can make noises to register pleasure or pain. But what differentiates man from beast, and civilisation from wilderness, is the use of articulated speech: logos… to a patriarchal social order like that of classical Greece, there is something abnormal about the use of signs to transcribe upon the outside of the body a meaning from inside the body which does not pass through the control point of logos.

Anne Carson – *The Gender of Sound*

One way to put off loneliness is to interpose God.

Anne Carson – *The Glass Essay*

And what kind of madness is it anyway to be in love with something constitutionally incapable of loving you back?

Maggie Nelson – *Bluets*

There is at times a magic in identity of position; it is one of those things that have suggested to us eternal comradeship

E. M. Forster – *A Room with a View*

To be noticed is to be loved

Ali Smith – *There But For The*

Foreword
Ed Madden, director

Two young aristocrats argue at the edge of an ocean. A Senate committee reckons with the sudden disappearance of all the fish in the sea. And a pair of scientists gaze at an octopus in a tank, and are gazed at in return. Let's address the whale in the room: why does Marek write marine plays?

Well, he grew up near the sea, and loved it, and loves it still; he loves to swim in it and to walk beside it, and he is prodigiously good at cooking things that come from it, too. In his flat there is a poster of the cover of Iris Murdoch's *The Sea, The Sea*; and also an octopus ice bucket I got him for his birthday. So, I do think a part of it is that, for Marek, to write about the ocean and the creatures that inhabit it is to spend time in an environment with which he has a deep physical and imaginative affinity. But more than that, his plays actually draw their impetus, their fuel, from the vastness, mystery and force of the sea; in each of *Wild Swimming, Yellowfin* and *Octopolis*, characters are thrown into relief by their relationship to the scale and unknowability of the ocean and/or the almost alien quality of its lifeforms. None of these plays are set *at sea* but its presence is felt as a richly flexible source of metaphorical context; look, too, at the tidal fluidity of the typography, the arrangement of words on the page, which does so much to say: *something is going on here, something liquid and slippery and alive*.

Octopolis is a play about perspective and attention and the extent to which we can ever hope to understand what's going on inside other people's heads, in which George and Harry's relationship is largely mediated through their scrutiny of an animal that has itself long been at the centre of extraordinary debates around consciousness, sentience and selfhood. It is a work of piercing intellectual curiosity and real heart; a study of two great minds who are also complex and wounded people, and whose investigation into the nature and scope of Frances the octopus' experience of the world gives rise to fundamental human questions of faith and feeling; brain, body and soul. It is a challenge and a pleasure to rehearse text that demands such ratiocinative and emotional acuity, and is so supplely theatrical.

In many ways, apparently, it's easier to travel to space than to the bottom of the sea; and by most estimates we have explored less than ten per cent of our oceans. The best of Marek's writing captures something of the way I feel when contemplating those unplumbed depths. Whether you are holding this playtext as an audience member or reader, or to stage it yourself, I wish you a measure of the stimulation, wonder, and thrill of discovery that it has brought me.

September 2023

Acknowledgements

My thanks to Jessica Stewart for putting me out there and for having my back; to the staff at the Hampstead Theatre for programming this play and for producing it with such spirited aplomb; to Jemma Redgrave and Ewan Miller for having the bravery to say yes and for being so incredibly good, and to Ed Madden – impeccable as always – for directing *Octopolis,* and for putting together such a fabulous and formidable team.

Thanks also to my friends for keeping me sane – especially Sam and Mim, my playwriting partners in crime – and to my family, Clans Chapman, Horn and Myers, for all their love, support and enthusiasm.

M.H.

This text went to press before the end of rehearsals and so may differ slightly from the play as performed.

Octopolis was first performed at Hampstead Theatre Downstairs, London, on 15 September 2023. The cast was as follows:

HARRY	Ewan Miller
GEORGE	Jemma Redgrave
Director	Ed Madden
Designer	Anisha Fields
Lighting	Jamie Platt
Sound	Esther Kehinde Ajayi
Movement and Intimacy	Angela Gasparetto

Characters

GEORGE, *an ethologist / a widow / a recluse*
HARRY, *an anthropologist / a loner / an interloper*
FRANCES, *an octopus*

A Note on the Staging

In The Past the dialogue is not embodied. Think about the relationship between what they are saying and what they are doing.

In A Future the dialogue is fully embodied, to the extent that it is not even spoken or, indeed, written.

Notes on the Text

Attends, Attend and *Attend* – Where there is an 's' on the end, this word should be pronounced as it would be in French: 'Tu attends.' If there is no 's' then 'Attend' should be pronounced the English way. Where italics are used on the English spelling this is a suggestion to the actor that they might want to lend special emphasis to that word.

Giscard – Although this is a French surname, my feeling is that Harry would've anglicised the pronunciation. He uses a hard 'G' (as in 'Give') and a hard 'D' (as in 'Lard').

A 'Pause' or a 'Beat' denotes a break in the rhythm of discourse. For clarity's sake a Beat is a shorter and more rhythmic Pause. A 'Silence', however short, suggests the absence of the desire to speak. Outside of these moments, this is a quick play, and the dialogue should move at a fair lick, otherwise we'll be here all day.

Traditional punctuation is not always adhered to at the point at which a line breaks. Rather, guidance regarding pace, rhythm and sense should be inferred from the line breaks themselves.

ACT ONE

A caption appears in the blueish darkness: A FUTURE.

GEORGE *and* HARRY *dance to David Bowie.*

The movements are small and tentative, precise and symmetrical.

*

A new caption appears: THE PAST. *Unless otherwise stated, it should remain for the duration of the act.*

H. She stood in the doorway

G. Jesus Christ!

H. It was apparent to me, for various reasons, that I must've woken her up

G. What the fuck do you think you're doing?

H. I'm sorry!

G. How the hell did you get in here?

H. This is the Octopus House, is it not? You are Professor Grey?

G. What are you doing with my kettle?

H. I'm...
Well, I'm making a cup of tea

G. *Right*

Beat.

H. Would you...

Like one?

G. No!

H. Right

.

G. *What I would like*
   Is to know why you're stood in my fucking kitchen
   Unannounced
   First thing in the fucking morning!

H. Professor, it is *not* first thing, it is nearly midday
   And it is not *your* kitchen

G. Well I'm sorry...

H. The kitchen, much like the kettle, *much like the rest of this house* belongs to the university

G. I'm sorry but this is a home invasion and I don't much feel like splitting hairs

H. *This is not a home invasion*

G. I don't much feel like swapping semantics with my fucking burglar, if it's all the same to you

H. I am not a burglar, I have a key
   I held the key above my head. My back was turned
   My eyes remained fixed upon the kettle and away from the doorway in which she stood

G. Well where the fuck did you get that!?

H. I'm sorry for the confusion
   I was assured everything had been arranged by the Director of Studies

G. The Director of Studies is a cunt

H. Right

G. I try to ignore the Director of Studies as best I can

H. Right
   Well then I think we might have discovered the source of our little misunderstanding, don't you?

G. Oh, fuck off

H. There should've been an email, professor, about the spare room
   Several emails

G. I don't read emails

H. Right

G. Certainly not the emails I receive from the Director of fucking Studies

H. Okay

G. And, regardless of what you may have been told about any such prospective vacancy, the debate is, *in the broadest sense of the term*, academic
There has been a mistake
There is no spare room for you to inhabit, theoretically or otherwise

H. She protested, and then, immediately

G. Oh
Oh, I suppose you mean John's study

Beat.

I'm sorry Mr...?

H. *Doctor*
Giscard

G. I'm sorry Doctor Giscard, when my husband was alive it was just the two of us
We had no need for the second bedroom so we...
Well... anyway

Pause. GEORGE *is lost in thought.*

H. ...Professor?

G. I'm actually still very much personally engaged in the research that my late husband and I were conducting before his death

H. I'm aware of that

G. Although, I admit, his recent passing has left me somewhat *waylaid*, I do not consider myself to be in need of an assistant
I apologise on behalf of the Director of Studies for the misunderstanding

H. That is not what is going on here, professor

G. The Director of Studies, who is a cunt, as I think I may have
   mentioned?

H. You did, yes

G. Should never have advertised the vacancy

H. Professor Grey, I am not here to assist you
   I'm here to conduct a research project of my own, concerning
   Frances

   Beat.

G. Oh
   I see

   Beat.

H. At the mention of the octopus some new colour entered her
   voice

G. You know, I think perhaps I will have that cup of tea, after all

H. I will make you a cup of tea, professor, and I promise I will
   explain everything
   But first
   Please
   Would you mind putting on some clothes?

   Beat.

   She took a moment to process my request
   She examined herself but was far from alarmed

G. Well yes, now you mention it
   It is a little chilly

   *

G. I went upstairs and dressed

   When I returned to the living room the flustered figure I'd
   met in the kitchen was transformed
   He was ramrod straight, stock still, utterly composed
   Staring into the large aquarium that dominated the space

He was clean and kempt in a fastidious, 'public school' kind of way
In a way that made him seem quite lonely

H. I took the initiative

G. He handed me a coffee

H. Thought you could do with waking up.

Beat.

G. Normally, she'd come and say hello but she's a little morose at the moment
She's wearing her widow's weeds, you see
This earned a delicate smile

H. You mean to say that your octopus is in mourning, Professor Grey?

G. There were three people in my marriage, Doctor Giscard
Three people and twelve legs
Thank you for the coffee

Beat.

You'll never find her. She's invisible
Well,
To the untrained eye, at least
At this, he smirked and turned his head

H. Alright then
Train me

Beat.

G. Hmm
My turn to smile

Beat.

Most molluscs have a shell to protect them from predation, but not Frances
By way of compensation, evolution has seen fit to make her a master of disguise

She can morph herself into any shape she chooses and the
pigment pouches in her skin mean that she can summon the
deep, speckled blue *of that rock*
Over there
At will

Beat.

H. Ah yes, there she is
Extraordinary

Pause.

G. There are certain people who are gifted with the power to
make a silence feel comfortable
He was not one of them
Of course, it's not just camouflage
They *communicate* through colour, too
In an elaborate and expressive form of semaphore
'I'm hungry', 'I'm horny', 'I'm scared'
'I'm angry'
'Lonely'
'Sad'

H. Right

G. More remarkable still is that they do it in isolation
Shifting from colour to colour when they don't even know
they're being watched

H. Talking to themselves, you mean?
Thinking aloud?

G. Yes
Exactly that

H. Fascinating

Pause.

I notice that you live in a state of squalor, Professor Grey

G. *Fucking hell*

H. It's just an observation

G. Christ, you're blunt!

H. No, I'm French. There's a difference

G. *French*?

H. Yes

G. You don't sound it

H. Well
   I am

G. Bullshit, you're as English as they come
   A stuffed-shirt, boy's-own-adventure-book, public-school,
   toffee-nosed *English* cunt
   I didn't say that last bit

H. Only on my mother's side, I'm afraid
   And I really do mean no offence. My concern is only for my
   work
   I'm afraid I cannot *work* in these conditions

G. That isn't my concern

H. Professor Grey

G. George
   My name is George

H. George, I respect your personal boundaries, your proclivities,
   your way of living
   Indeed, it is a *central tenet* of my own field of study that I do
   precisely that
   But, surely to God, this room is uninhabitable

G. On the contrary, Doctor Giscard

H. Harry, please

G. On the contrary, *Harry*, Frances and I inhabit it just fine

H. Frances *inhabits* her tank

G. Try telling her that

   Beat.

This is our den
We share it, Frances and I
She has her corner and I have mine
I gestured to where I'd pulled two sofas into parallel lines,
back to back with a space in between
A duvet slung over the top, with another one acting as a
ground sheet
He stared at me, again
That deep, implacable stare
And then that lupine grin

H. I'm afraid I don't understand

G. No, I thought
No you don't
And it's *fucking killing you*

*

H. She used her whole body when she spoke, as if she were
thinking through movement
Sharp paroxysms and soft undulations of torso, arm, neck
and head
Not just *punctuating* thought but *actually aiding* in the
summoning of ideas

G. Our field of study was animal culture
By which I mean the *social* rather than *genetic* transfer of
information
How a fish knows how to swim, for example, is *genetically*
encoded, whereas how a monkey knows to open nuts with a
rock is learned through observation
As such, research within our field was limited, at that time, to
animals that live in groups
Octopuses, by way of contrast, are not only solitary but
actually notoriously hostile
Even breeding pairs are as likely to eat each other as they are
to successfully mate

H. Sounds like my ex-wife, I said
She ignored me

G. And so, despite demonstrating a level of cognition that is equal to that of high-level primates, they remained overlooked
Until, that is, something happened which turned all such received wisdom on its head

H. She paused, for dramatic emphasis
This was clearly the 'stump speech'

G. A few years ago, a couple of hours' sail out of Sydney Harbour, an amateur deep-sea diver discovered a large pile of scallop shells arranged shambolically on the seabed
As the diver looked more closely he noticed some movement, and so he waited

Beat.

Slowly
Gradually
Presumably having made the assessment that he posed no threat
Something close to *two dozen* octopuses emerged from out of the mound of shells

H. She talked of her work as though no one had ever heard of it

G. When he made his findings public
When he revealed the place he called *Octopolis* to the world
It sent a shockwave through the academic community

H. Here she was
The great George Grey

G. It wasn't that these creatures had begun to behave as a pride or a herd or a flock, you understand

H. I don't mind admitting that I was star-struck

G. Rather, what the experts were bearing witness to was a kind of *contingent* cohabitation that was thought unique to the human world
Neither friends nor enemies, these octopuses had unwittingly built for themselves a kind of begrudging non-community

H. I've had a few flatshares like that, I said
   Thinking she'd ignore me again, but no
   She looked at me
   Really looked

G. Yes
   Yes a flatshare is *exactly* right

H. Hmmm, I thought
   One gold star to me

G. Now, as all this was happening, John and I were becoming
   increasingly interested in what we called 'interspecies
   cultural transfer'
   Not just the transfer of information *within* herds and flocks
   and prides but *between,* say, humans and other kinds of high-
   cognition animals
   What if, we wondered, you took a creature of acute cognitive
   capacity and...
   Well, sort of... 'gifted' it the human world in all its richness?

   Beat.

   Octopolis was the necessary catalyst for this work because
   it showed that an octopus's unique and dazzling intelligence
   could be, in some way, harnessed
   It could be manipulated and enriched through socialisation
   Through *enculturation*
   And that is when we began to work on the Octopus House

H. This doesn't explain why you choose to sleep on the floor of
   your living room

G. Yes it does

H. No
   It doesn't

G. Yes
   It does
   Because that duvet over there is my scallop shell, Harry
   Just as, when my husband was dying and he couldn't get up
   the stairs any more, the bed he slept in, in that corner there,
   that was *his* scallop shell

Frances doesn't have a shell but she has her rock
And, although the mess and the clutter of this room
might seem highly objectionable to your more fastidious
tendencies,
To Frances and myself it represents nothing less than
the slow accretion of cultural detritus that typifies the
interspecies shared experience

Beat. HARRY *thinks*.

H. Some of this was obviously bollocks
The ravings, quite frankly, of a mad woman
But on some barely conscious level I intuited something
important in what she was saying
This was all much more relevant to my own sphere of
interest than I had erstwhile understood

Beat.

Alright fine, you make a good case
The living room can remain as it is on one condition

G. This isn't a negotiation

H. I get full use of both the remaining bedroom *and* your late
husband's study

G. No

H. Why not?

G. Because why should I?
I could go straight to the office of the Director of Studies and
having you billeted elsewhere

H. No you couldn't

G. Why couldn't I?

H. Because I need to be here

G. That's not my problem

H. Right, and how much influence do you suppose you hold,
right now, at this current moment, over the Director of
Studies?

How much *leverage* do you think you have?
You who has stopped teaching?
Stopped writing?
Stopped publishing papers, making media appearances or
even deigning to answer her boss's emails?
Either you're a leading public intellectual or a professional
recluse, you can't be both

G. I'm grieving

H. There are limits

G. Yes there are, but I still hold sway

H. Not as much as me

G. Really?

H. Yes

G. Well I've never heard of you

H. Not yet, but you will
Everyone will
Because if what I think is happening is happening then I have
something in my back pocket which is worth ten times more
to this institution than whatever loose ends of yours and your
husband's it is that they've left you here, *under sufferance*, to
tidy up

Beat.

In fact, I would go one further
I would venture that the only reason that they are still
tolerating your continued presence here *at all* is, actually,
because of what *I* know
And what I *want* to know
And what I *will go on* to know before I am finished here

Pause.

G. I think it's time you showed your hand
Don't you?

Beat.

H. I'm an anthropologist
I'm here to observe you and Frances and your, as you put it,
'interspecies shared experience'

G. And why should I consent to that?

H. Because if you don't then they'll pull your funding and close
you down

G. Right
Charming

H. And, because I think you'll want to know
When I tell you what it is that I'm here to find out, I think
you'll want to know, too

Beat.

Put simply, George
I am here to ascertain whether or not your octopus believes
in God

*

G. He left the room, heading back into the kitchen, before
returning with two huge suitcases
Would you like a hand with those?

H. Not with these, no
But the others, perhaps

G. Whilst he comported himself like a resourceful Boy Scout,
he packed like a minor royal
By the time I'd dragged the rest upstairs, he was laying out
his jackets
Onto the bed that John and I had shared

H. It's very simple,
It all goes back to Victorian England, the imperial project and
the birth of the secular society

G. He criss-crossed the room
Laying claim
Gosh, really? As simple as that?

H. Although changes in the discourse since that time have been
   seismic, the findings of anthropology's early practitioners
   still speak to the way we live now
   They identified a near-ubiquitous tendency for cultures to
   evolve through three key stages, defined by three governing
   theories of how the universe functions
   All societies start, they explained, with a theory of magic
   Which is then superseded by a theory of religion
   Which is then superseded by a theory of science

G. He was now unpacking several pairs of shorts and some thin
   linen shirts
   This horrified me
   It was, after all, November

H. Imagine a small tribe with a rudimentary grasp of the basics
   of agriculture
   They grow, let's say, tomato plants
   Late one night, a member of this tribe gets drunk, goes out
   and takes a piss on the plants and the next day it rains
   It rains and rains and the tomatoes grow plump and healthy
   Subsequently, this strange event is *rationalised* through an
   anthropocentric lens
   'It must have been the pissing', it is reasoned, 'that made the
   rain come'
   Status is thusly conferred upon this drunken fool, a new
   hierarchy is established and entrenched and this, George, is
   the essence of shamanism
   This is how a society develops a governing Theory of Magic

G. With insufferable detachment, he flung another case on to the
   bed

H. Now, in order to move from magic to religion you need to
   irrevocably frustrate this narrative of cause and effect
   A drought, say, which precipitates the death of the plants and
   the hunger of the tribe and which no amount of drinking and
   pissing seems able to alleviate
   And yet, it is reasoned, *someone* must have made the rain
   come
   Someone

Somewhere
Elsewhere
And, since the rain came from the sky, it is reasoned that 'the man who makes the rain come' must live there
Eventually someone comes forward, claiming to be able to *intercede* with this sky-living, rain-bringer and this man is a priest

Beat.

Perhaps, once a year, a ritual is performed
A small wooden model of a tomato plant is wheeled out, and this priest splashes holy piss-substitute oil on the figurine in front of a devoted congregation
Perhaps this is done, George, to secure a bountiful crop and the salvation of the community
And this, in very simple terms, is how a theory of magic is superseded by a...

G. Fascinating stuff, Harry, really
But what's it got to do with my octopus?

Beat.

For the first time, now, there was an apprehensiveness about him

H. I read your latest paper
I found it very moving

Pause.

G. Something should be said about this
It requires, I feel, further explication

*

A caption reads: BEFORE. *It is present for the duration of this scene, replacing* THE PAST.

G. In the Animal Kingdom, food-related hierarchies, etiquettes and rituals are a central organising feature of any developed cultural unit that one might care to mention
With this in mind, a game was devised around Frances's mealtimes to see whether she could learn a set of rules and

In so doing
Exhibit behaviours which were suggestive of the kind of
social learning that we were looking for
Now…

H. Now, in order to accurately assess an animal's cognitive
capacity you have to account for its physiological strengths
and weaknesses
What behavioural biologists call its 'umwelt'
As such, the 'game' which Professor Grey…
…The *other* Professor Grey
Professor *John* Grey devised was one that made particularly
good use of Frances's deft ability to change colour

G. Borrowing the spinning wheel from an old Twister set, John
would sit next to the tank with a bucket of defrosted crab
He'd turn the arrow towards the colour which most closely
resembled Frances at that moment
He'd show her the wheel
And then he'd feed her

H. Next, he started spinning the arrow first
He would then wait until Frances, having made the
associative leap herself, turned the colour upon which the
needle landed

G. Finally, John made it harder still by repeatedly re-spinning
the wheel every time Frances shifted to the corresponding
hue
Frances would have to change to the new colour eight times
in a row to secure her meal
This game, its progression, and Frances's swinging emotional
state from curiosity to boredom to outrage and back to
curiosity again
Was, in the main, the subject of the article

Pause.

H. Yes, but there was also a tantalising coda
Wasn't there?

Beat.

G. After John died I wasn't thinking straight
   I wasn't sleeping
   I wasn't eating

H. And so, consequently, neither was Frances

   Beat.

G. Days went by
   Almost a week
   When I eventually remembered, I rushed into the kitchen to get a bag of crabs
   At the sight of which, Frances shot out from under her rock and up into the middle of the tank
   Her head, or rather, her hood pointing towards the floor

H. And she wasn't blue or green or yellow or red?
   She wasn't any of the colours on the wheel at all?

G. No
   She was the brightest orange

H. And has she ever gone blue or green or yellow or red, when confronted with a crab or a colour wheel, since?

G. No. Only orange

H. Right. And why might that be significant?

   Beat.

   Go on

G. Because orange was John's favourite colour

H. And what did you call this behaviour, George?
   At the very end of your incredible essay?

   Beat.

G. I wasn't in my right mind
   I wasn't being *objective*

H. George

G. Grief
   I used the word 'grief'

*

The caption, again, reads: THE PAST.

G. Moving? You found it *moving*?

H. Yes. I did
   I continued my unpacking

G. Well I think that's a very odd reaction

H. Yes well, perhaps that's because you don't truly understand
   the wider implications of what you wrote
   At this she smirked

G. Right. Sure
   If you say so

   Beat.

H. There was now, to my mind, a glimmer of something new in
   her
   She seemed distracted
   Haunted
   Hunted

   Beat.

   George... spinning that wheel
   Letting the needle rest at random
   That behaviour would've seemed, *from Frances's
   perspective*, as capricious as a raincloud
   Consequently, her response was no different from that of the
   village shaman
   Pissing on his tomatoes and hoping for the best

G. Bullshit
   She'd merely learned to do as she was told
   He span the wheel and she changed colour

H. Yes, but *from her perspective,* George
   What's to say that, *in her mind*, going the *preceding* colour
   didn't 'summon' the *proceeding* spin?
   And the next one, and the next, until shifting colours and
   spinning wheels summoned the crab?

G; But she didn't 'summon' the next colour!
   My husband did that when he span the wheel

H. Again
   George
   Try telling her that

   Pause.

G. Alright fine, but even if that were the case

H. Where does God come in to it?

G. Yes!

H. A fair question

G. Because *religion*, Harry, a belief in an *actual God* is a little
   more complicated than that

H. I'm aware of that

G. That requires something more

H. Yes, it requires the sublimation of agency and the
   transference of authority from magician to deity and for that
   to happen there needs to be some kind of cataclysm
   In the example of the shaman and the tomato plants the
   inciting incident is the drought
   In Frances's case it was John's death, your depression and,
   subsequently, the empty bucket, devoid of crab
   Suddenly, *from Frances's perspective*, no amount of colour
   conjuring can bring the crab back
   Suddenly, it is *no longer in Frances's power* to make the
   magic wheel spin
   Suddenly it becomes clear to her that this power *actually
   always rested* elsewhere
   With John,
   With the strange alien creature who is no longer there on the
   other side of the glass

   Beat.

   And so she devises a way of continuing to communicate with
   John despite his absence and the solution she lands on is
   Ritual Action
   Every day, without fail, the same strange act of supplication
   Never again 'playing the game'

Beat.

That bright-orange colouration you described, along with the
drooping tentacles and the upturned hood? That is a prayer,
George
A prayer to your late husband
The Great Crab-God

Beat.

G. You're insane

H. You have already said that you believe octopuses to be
capable of thinking through colour
And grieving through colour
Why should they not be capable of praying through colour,
too?

G. That's fucking mental

H. Why?

G. Because that's not how animals work!

H. She was angry now
It gave her a kind of vibrancy

G. Law,
History,
Mathematics,
Art,
Science,
God
These *abstractions* are in the singular possession of the
human animal because their conception and evolution
requires the use of complex and multifaceted thought
structures and sign systems
They require, however rudimentary it might be, forms of
language
It is impossible to create, develop and sustain such language
systems without recourse to something which only the human
animal, as far as we know, has ever shown any facility with

H. Which is what?

G. Tools

H. *Yes*

G. The making and using of sophisticated, specific-utility tools
Tools which aid expression and help to record things and to
build things
Whether that means building temples and shrines, or whether
that means building the *ideas* that underpin and inspire such
monuments, the principle remains resolutely the same

H. I am aware of this, Professor Grey

G. Frances doesn't make tools, *Doctor Giscard*, so she can't
make signs
If she can't make signs then she can't make *sign systems*
If she can't make sign systems then she can't have symbolic
culture
And if she can't have symbolic culture then she can't pray
to an Octopus God any more than she can paint an Octopus
Mona Lisa or write a Declaration of Octopus Independence
It's as simple as that
Game over

Pause.

H. Consider, as your husband did, Frances's 'umwelt'
Specifically, the expressive dexterity of her camouflage
function
Frances doesn't need tools, George
…Because she already is one

Beat.

She is the world's best Swiss-army knife
A box of the finest St Petersburg watercolours
And the most powerful image-mapping software known to
man
All rolled into one
Saying that an octopus can't '*express itself*' because it
doesn't use '*tools*' is like saying a snake can't move because
it doesn't have legs

The snake just wriggled over and bit you, *professor*
The octopus just prayed to your Crab-God Dead Husband!

Beat.

Having packed away most of my things into a vacant set of
drawers I moved across the room to the wardrobe
With a triumphant flourish, I flung the doors wide
Only to be confronted with another man's clothes

Pause.

G. Can you stop unpacking actually?

H. I'm sorry

G. Can you stop unpacking and just stop *fucking* talking for one
fucking minute!?

H. ....*George*

G. I really would like to clear some of John's stuff away, if
that's alright?
Get shit organised before you start *making yourself at home*,
if it's all the same to you?

H. Yes
Of course

G. If it's all the same to you, I'd like you to leave this room,
now, actually, please

H. Alright
Of course
That's fine

G. Now!
Please!

*

G. He went downstairs
Eventually I followed
Returning to the living room as he emerged from the kitchen

H. You don't have any food
Your cupboards are bare

G. He was eerily detached
   As though nothing had happened

   Beat.

   I removed a menu from under a pile of papers on the coffee
   table and held it up to the tank
   It had photos, which was handy
   That's because we order in

   Beat.

   Deliberating for a moment, as suspicious of him as I was,
   eventually Frances emerged
   When she was finally close enough, she extended a tentacle
   over the top of tank and towards the card
   Yellowfin sashimi
   Good choice

   Beat.

   I handed him the leaflet
   I'll have what she's having

H. You're going out?

G. I need a walk
   I couldn't look at him
   I left

   Beat.

   When I returned, he was nibbling at a California roll
   Silently, I picked up a piece of sockeye salmon and took it
   towards the tank
   I felt four eyes upon me and, suddenly, Frances flared into
   life
   Huge and vibrantly coloured

H. Is that it?

G. He was close beside me now

H. Is that the orange colouration as you described it in your
   paper?

G. No, I said
   No, that's red
   And I looked at the wheel, discarded on the floor
   And I saw where the arrow was pointed
   And I realised that, for the first time in months, Frances was
   playing the game

Beat.

It's good that you're not a light packer, Doctor Giscard
Because it looks like you might be here for some time

ACT TWO

A caption appears in the blueish darkness: A FUTURE.

GEORGE *and* HARRY *dance to a (maybe different?) song by David Bowie.*

The movements are more elaborate but still precise and symmetrical; building on what came before.

*

A new caption appears: THE PAST. *It should remain for the duration of the act.*

H. It is only in retrospect that I can appreciate how extraordinary
    it was for George to leave the house that afternoon
    Over the next few weeks it became increasingly clear that
    George does not leave
    George stays put

   Beat.

   In that respect she was much like her octopus
   Frances, too, would sit, sullenly, under her rock
   Never once blooming into the blistering orange that George
   had described in print

   Beat.

   Endless days of attritional silence left me wanting to scream
   I would try to make basic conversation
   What are you reading? I might ask

G.…A book

H. She might reply
    Any good? I'd press on

G.…*Nope*

   Beat.

H. Otherwise, I might attempt to introduce some basic precepts
of domestic propriety
One morning I took a punt in informing her that we were
Out of milk again, George

G. Yes, sorry about that. I like it on my muesli

H. No George, you don't, you like it on *my* muesli
Which, by the way, is also something that we're now running
low on

G. And teabags

H. Sorry?

G. We're out of teabags too
For when you next go shopping, I mean

Beat.

H. And that wasn't the worst of it. Far from it

Beat.

One morning, unable to sleep, I came downstairs early to
make a cup of tea
I knew she did yoga at sunrise quite religiously, but what
I failed to anticipate was that
Much like that first morning we met
It might not occur to her to get dressed properly first

G. Whoops
Sorry

H. Oh for fuck's sake!

G. Forgot you were here, I'm afraid

H. This is a communal space, George! You can't just do what
you like any more!

G. I'm in my own home, aren't I?

H. No! You're not!
This is university property. It's a workplace. There are rules!

G. Oh why do you have to be so *fucking bourgeois* about
everything?
Honestly, you're supposed to be French

H. I stormed back upstairs
I could hear her shouting after me

G. I thought you were supposed to engage in the cultural life of
the tribe, Harry?
We can always roll out another mat for you
There's plenty of room!

Beat.

H. I spent the rest of the day packing, unpacking and repacking
my things
I knew, in my heart, that I had failed to ingratiate myself,
would continue to do so and would most likely go mad from
trying
And yet
When I went downstairs that evening, to announce my
departure
I found George kneeling
In the dark
Very close to the tank and muttering under her breath

Beat.

The only sound that could be heard was the clicking of a
rosary, as the beads moved briskly between her fingers
Click, click, click, they went
Click
Click
Click

Beat.

It was an image that did not yet make sense to me
But it was too arresting,
Too alluring, too uncanny, too strange to be ignored
And I knew that I must stay

*

G. He would pace, endlessly
Doing laps of the living room

Beat.

I know Homes under the Hammer isn't the most taxing of
intellectual conceits, Harry, but that doesn't mean you're not
being fucking distracting

H. Is it feeding time yet?

G. You know it isn't
You need to relax

H. If she won't do what I've come to see then what is the point
of me being here?

G. Bloody good question

H. Oh don't start!

G. You've read the paper
I don't see why you can't just draw your conclusions from
that

H. That isn't how it works

G. I don't see why not
My descriptions were perfectly accurate

H. Your descriptions were partial
Subjective
Biased

G. I am still a professional scientist, you know, despite
appearances
It is still my job to be empirical
He moved. Placing himself between me and the screen
Oi!

H. Your paper doesn't constitute ethnographic data, George,
because you're not Frances's anthropologist
You could only ever give a partial, *and misleading*, account
because you are, yourself, a member of the cultural unit that
requires study
And so it's absolutely fine for you to pick your toenails and
make endless cups of tea and watch Cash in the fucking Attic
all day, because that's all still data
That's all still, in its own meagre, depressing way, a kind of
culture…

G. Gosh you really can be devastatingly charming, you know that?

H. But it doesn't *mean* very much if Frances won't do her ever-so-special party trick for her Uncle Harry!

Beat.

I have to see what I came here to see with my own eyes and I am not leaving until I do

Quietly.

G. Well that's a shame then, isn't it, because you don't stand a fucking chance

H. I'm sorry?

Beat.

G. I said
That you don't stand
A fucking chance

Beat.

Look at the way she looks at you
Even now, whilst you rant and rave and curse her name like she's not in the fucking room
Look at the *quality* of that attention
You've barely met her gaze more than half a dozen times since you got here, and that's much less than she deserves and she *knows* it

H. Well then help me to make her see that I'm worthy of her time!

G. *No*

H. No?
What do you mean no?

G. This has got nothing to do with me, Harry

H. The sooner I see what I came here to see, the sooner I'll be out of your life

G. Yes well, as enticing a proposition as that surely is, some things are more important

H. Like what?!

Beat.

Like what, George?

Beat.

G....Like Cash in the *fucking* Attic

A pause that fades into a silence.

I turned back to the television and he stood looking
helplessly into the tank for several minutes
I couldn't tell him yet why I didn't want to help him, because
I didn't yet know it myself
And so instead the question hung there, torturing us both

Beat.

And then something *shifted*
All of a sudden, he was across the room
He retrieved a chair from behind the dining table and placed
it by the side of the tank
He rolled up his sleeve
He climbed on the chair
And he plunged his hand in

H. Fuck, that's cold!

G. That's more like it, I thought

Pause.

Even so, after standing like that for the best part of an hour,
his patience began, once again, to fray

H. This is hopeless

G. No it isn't, I found myself saying
Stay where you are and stick at it

H. Most days, she won't come out from underneath that rock if I
am even in the room

G. You have to give her your time and your attention and you
have to give it freely
You have to learn to *attend* to her, Harry

Pause.

H. In French...
   The word 'Attends' is an injunction, meaning 'wait'

G. Well there you are,
   'Attends', Harry
   Attend and Attends. Watch and wait
   But do it *actively* and with an intensity that feels like love
   Notice her, Harry
   Alright?

   Beat. GEORGE *and* HARRY *notice each other, properly –*
   perhaps for the first time

   I was up, now, standing beside and beneath him on that
   ridiculous chair
   I had a momentary urge, almost irresistible, to wrap myself
   around his leg

   Beat.

   And then, suddenly, there she was
   She bobbed towards us, took a chance, and lurched for
   Harry's hand

H. Her touch
   It's so
   Tender

   Silence.

G. Why bother?

H. What do you mean?

G. Well...
   Even if you *could* prove that it's all, on some level, 'true',
   what would that mean?
   What would be *the point* of that?

   Beat.

   He thought for a second, as two more tentacles crept up his
   arm
   Toying with the undone buttons of his hastily rolled sleeve

H. In 1970 an album called Songs of the Humpback was
     released into the US charts
     Within two years whale hunting was banned in the United
     States
     That is what happened when the American public learned
     that animals could sing, George
     So what do you think might happen if they learned that they
     could pray?
     What would happen if they learned that they had souls?

   Beat.

   If I can prove as much then perhaps I can confront the
   abiding fiction of a Christian moral order that separates
   humanity from the rest of the animal kingdom
   Perhaps I can provoke the kind of drastic *spiritual*
   reorientation that is necessary for us to save us from
   ourselves
   Perhaps, George, I can help to save the world

   Beat.

G. All eight tentacles whirled and unfurled around his arm now
     In an intense and undulating full-body caress

   Beat.

   You're a maniac

H. No, I'm not
     I'm just right, in a way you find terrifying

G. Yes, well, that is *exactly* what a messianic psychopath *would*
     say, I'm afraid

H. Yes, and that is exactly what a person who felt fundamentally
     threatened would say in turn

G. I don't feel threatened by you

H. Don't you?
     Really?
     Someone who keeps wild animals in captivity for research
     purposes fails to feel 'seen'
     In any way

By the contention that our self-entitled covetousness is destroying the natural world?

G. Frances isn't my chattel, Harry
I don't enjoy 'dominion' over her, if that's what you're getting at

H. George, you literally keep her in a tank in your living room

G. I smiled
He smiled
We were...
I guess the word would be...
Enjoying
Ourselves

Beat.

Yes, well, you're the one whose entire academic discipline is born out of the parasitic, condescending *and fundamentally colonial* practice of wandering off round the globe poking your nose into the business of what you term 'primitive cultures'
So
You know

H. That is not what we do

G. ....People in glass houses, Harry

H. That is not the word we use, not any more

G. It's the word they used though, isn't it?
Your *illustrious* Victorian forbears

H. *They were a product of their time*

G. Oh yes
Well we've all heard that one before, haven't we?
Covers all manner of sins, doesn't it?

H. Yes, well those who seek to dismiss them are a product of their time too
Nobody escapes the social facts of the culture into which they are born, George, *nobody*

G. Still, I think it's important to recognise when advances have
been made

H. Oh don't be so moronic, cultures don't 'advance'

G. Excuse me, *moronic*?

H. They don't advance and they cannot be 'perfected' and woe
betide anyone who tries
Culture isn't something we *make*. It's just something that
happens to us
It's *trauma*
We don't learn by 'doing', we learn by being fucked up!
We get fucked into certain ways of behaving and we mould
ourselves accordingly because truthfully
On an evolutionary level
Nobody likes feeling left out
It's as simple and pathetic as that

G. Well I think that's fucking cynical

H. Well yes of course you do
Of course you *would*
Because you're the great George Grey!
The great independent thinker
The great recluse!
But even here, even in your profound and singular grief
Even having carved out a role for yourself as the strange
Philosopher-Queen of your own private wilderness
Even here you are not immune from the ravages of the
culture into which you were born
Because even the very grief upon which you subsist is a
social construct

G. *Harry*

H. And the performance of that grief *most definitely* is

G. Harry!

H. You think you're sad because your husband died but you're
not, George. You're not
You're sad because the culture you were born into told you
that you *should be*

Your 'sadness' is as culturally mandated as anything else and
that's it

G. Harry, enough!

Beat. The temperature changes.

H. Fuck. I'm sorry

G. Fuck you

H. I shouldn't have said that

G. *Fuck*
You

H. I wasn't thinking. It just slipped out
I'm a cunt, I'm sorry

G. I moved away

H. I'm sorry!

G. He went to get down off the chair, but Frances was still
attached
He yanked his arm away, harshly, and
Suddenly
As quickly as she came
She was gone
Away, and under her rock

*

H. Days went by without speaking
I'd given up hope until, one morning, I came downstairs to
find her doing yoga
This time fully clothed
There was a familiar silence and then…

G. I've been thinking about what happened the other day

H. She was in an extended child's pose
Face on the floor, voice muffled
Sorry?

G. I've been thinking
About what happened the other day

H. She repeated, coming into table
Oh yes?

G. Yes

H. Up into a plank
Down into cobra
Long pause

Beat.

Look, George, I'm really sorry. I overstepped the mark and…

G. When David Bowie died I remember watching the news on
television
I remember them showing a clip from the music video for
'Lazarus'

H. Downward dog into three-legged dog

Beat.

…Right?

G. The reporter had registered the irony of this, you see
And he made a point of saying how, whereas Lazarus rose
from the dead, David Bowie would not
And I found myself thinking
'We don't know that though, do we?'
'We don't know what he'll do next'
And
I meant it
On some deep, irrational level I really *meant* it
And I cannot help but think that the reason we're all still so
quietly, disconsolately sad about the death of David Bowie is
not because he was so beautiful or talented or because he had
so much more to give
But rather
I think we're all just secretly a little confused as to why he
hasn't yet come back
And I guess what I mean by all this is…
Is that I think I understand better now why I didn't come to
your aid more quickly, with Frances

I think, on a basic level, the reason I didn't help is, well...
Because I believe in God

Beat.

H. Mountain, into tree into eagle
Sorry, George, I think I'm losing the thread of this slightly

G. Which is not to say that I think David Bowie *is* God
But just that, for many people, he filled the space where God
used to be

H. ...Back to tree

G. Perfectly rational people
People who would readily identify as atheists
Speaking for weeks afterwards in reverent tones about the
Star Man, returned to the stars
The Man Who Fell to Earth, gone home at last
This is the language of apotheosis, Harry
This is the language of ascension
And I guess what I ended up thinking was
What if *that's* it?
What if the *compulsion to believe* is, *in itself*, the very best
evidence that we have of God's presence?
What if it is God, Himself, who compels us, again and again,
to make room in our hearts for his substitutes on earth?
Even as we deny His existence, all the while

H. Mountain again, into tree, second side
Forward fold and then back into table
...*Right*

G. My husband was a Catholic
For him science and religion were not mutually exclusive and
when he lay dying in his bed I prayed by his side every night
and we both found comfort in that
And his faith became my faith, too
And so I can't want what you want, Harry
Not for me and not for John
I can't want you to find what it is that you want to find
Because if it can be proven that an *octopus* has been induced
into a belief in God then that belief can't have been given, by

God, to man
Rather, it might just be the result of some as-yet-unidentified
evolutionary process that suits an octopus just as well as it
suits us
And that would be that, again
The triviality of man's will to believe would be exposed,
again
And God would die, for me, all over again
And I can't want that

Beat.

I might be able to *accept* it, should you be able to *prove* it but
I cannot *want* it
And I think that has implications for how we are with one
another and so I wanted you to know

H. She was lying down now
    A hand on the belly and a hand on the heart
    Feet together, knees apart,
    The pose known as reclining bound angel

G. I wanted you to know that I am not on your side
    Because I think that has implications
    I think that means
    Most likely
    As a result

H. She gestured towards the tank

G....that she probably isn't either

*

*The song from the top of the act plays, but the source of the
sound is specific and tinny, as if coming from a radio.*

HARRY *dances the shuffling, distracted dance of someone
who is cooking someone else dinner, after a glass or two of
wine.*

The lights flick down to blueish darkness.

*

The lights flick up.

G. I'd been taking a long, mid-afternoon bath
Going downstairs, I was greeted by the most extraordinary
aromas and the sound of a radio, playing music
What are you doing? I asked

H. What does it smell like I'm doing?

G. He shouted through to me from the kitchen

H. I'm cooking

G. Head poking round the doorway

H. You remember cooking, right?

G. He came towards me with a glass of cold white wine

H. Take that

G. Thanks

H. And eat these

G. A small warm dish of... well I didn't know what they were

H. Panko-crumbed, pan-fried cod cheeks with wasabi mayo
Something to keep you quiet whilst I prep the razor clams

G. He turned to go back into the kitchen
Is this some kind of trap?

H. George
Come on
I'm French and I'm cooking you dinner
Of course it's a trap

G. He left the room and shouted back

H. I'm bored George
I'm bored of being treated like the enemy
Like an invading force that must be repelled
You don't agree with what I am doing here

G. Back again

H. And that's fine

But that doesn't mean that we can't get along

G. I looked at my plate
I didn't even know cod *had* cheeks

Beat.

Twenty minutes later and we're eating our main course

H. The shells aren't edible but everything else is. The green is
samphire

G. I tasted it
I ate a bit more and a bit more
And then
Suddenly
Fuck, sorry

H. George?

G. Sorry, I'm making you uncomfortable

H. No of course not but…
For God's sake, why are you crying?

G. It's all just
Very kind

Beat.

Two bottles later, and we're still in situ
The candles, now, just puddles of wax

H. I wrote my PhD on the coastal foraging communities of
Celtic Brittany
Known locally there as *Les Glaneurs*
Glaneur having the same root as the English verb 'to glean'
They pick mussels and rake for cockles and they also forage
for razor clams
The clams live in little burrows in the sand, and so to harvest
them you have to walk along the shoreline at low tide and
pour salt into the neat little holes that indicate their presence

G. Salt?

H. Table salt, yes

Some say that it acts as an irritant
Others that it tricks the clam into thinking the tide has come
in
Either way, suddenly, a long, slippery tuber-shaped shell
emerges, vertically, out of the sand
Which, naturally, you have to grab

G. Right
Well that sounds highly suggestive

H. You have to grab it and hold on for dear life because the
muscle that sits inside the shell
The thing you're eating now
That wants to escape your grasp

G. Yes, I've had that before

H. Right, well you mustn't take it personally
He's just frightened that you're going to eat him

G. I've had that a few times too

H. Look, do you want to know how to harvest razor clams or do
you want to make crass innuendos all evening?

G. Sorry
I'm listening
Sorry
I'm hanging on
I'm holding tight

H. Yes
Exactly
Don't let him get away

G. Okay

H. But it's a delicate balance, you see?

G. Right, of course

H. Because whilst you *must* grip on tightly, you must also try to
avoid pulling too hard

G. Right

H. A rule of thumb that, admittedly, may or may not be transferable to other scenarios

G. I see
And now who's making jokes?

H. Don't tug too hard, George

G. Yes, yes. Very funny

H. If you tug too hard then you risk ripping the muscle in half

G. Ah now you see that *hasn't* happened to me before

H. Are you sure?

G. Yes, I think I would know if I'd done that

H. Okay well then that is good news because otherwise half your dinner stays in the sand

Beat.

Just hold it, strong and steady and, eventually, the muscle will atrophy
The clam will be a spent force
And everything will go limp

G. Of course

H. And then you can pull your prey up and out and into your waiting bucket

G. Lovely
Very satisfying, I'm sure

Silence.

So, did they teach you to cook like that? These *'Gleaners'* of yours?

H. No, my father taught me
He was a chef in the kitchens of the college where my mother was doing her doctorate

G. She was an academic?

H. Yes, all her life

G. Mine too
   Taught classics at Cambridge

H. Gosh, well
   That sounds like a very similar set-up

G. Yes
   It does

   Silence.

   I remember I used to go bird watching on the Great Fen
   When I got home I'd tell Mum everything I'd seen and if
   I mentioned some species about which she had a classical
   anecdote she'd regale me with it
   Alcyone's kingfisher
   Leda's swan
   That sort of thing

   Beat.

   Gods turning into animals to get closer to humans
   Humans turned into animals because they got too close to the
   gods
   In Greek mythology the lines are very much blurred but for
   me those distinctions are supposed to be sacred

   Beat.

   Christ, I'm a fucking charlatan

H. No

G. A grieving octopus?
   It's ludicrous

H. You saw what you thought you saw. That's the end of it

G. Yes, but did I?
   Did I?

   Beat.

   I've spent my life searching out consciousness, Harry
   An entire career dedicated to identifying the moment
   at which an animal's base cognition ignites into a fuller
   awareness of *self*

And if I have learned anything from that
Anything at all
It's that it is a story

Beat.

Why we did the thing we did
Why we scratched that itch or ate that biscuit
Why we betrayed that trust and fucked that boy
These are the tales that we tell ourselves later, not decisions
we make in the here and now
Because there is no here and now, Doctor Giscard
The present does not exist
The present
The *actual* most 'now' moment of now is just...
...*Neurons*
Just twitches and impulses to which we retroactively ascribe
meaning
You say that Frances is sentient enough to pray and I say
she's not, but the truth is that both those conclusions sit
within a complex web of motives and agendas and the fact is
that it's all just probably bullshit
We act, in the moment, on impulse
We don't think, we just feel
We don't *choose*, we just do
And we're all really just about sentient enough to regale
ourselves with the anecdote, after the fact

Suddenly, HARRY *kisses* GEORGE.

Beat.

He does it again. GEORGE *pulls away.*

Why did you do that?

H. I don't know
From what you were saying, it felt like...

G. Right, yes
I see
I see

Beat.

H. I'm sorry, I just…

G. No, no, of course
   Of course you did

   Silence and then, maybe, music.

   And then the tank begins to glow.

H. Her hand moved across the table and towards his
   The smallest finger to the extreme right furtively caressed his
   knuckle

G. He turned his palm face up

H. Palm to palm

G. Fingers clasped around each other's

H. And they stayed that way for a very long time

G. And he did not look at her once

   Beat.

H. And then she released her grip, picked up a half-eaten razor
   clam and walked towards the tank

G. She looked at me
   I looked at him

H. And then I turned myself upside down

G. And with a flash

H. All of a sudden

G. I was the brightest possible orange

ACT THREE

A caption appears in the blueish darkness: A FUTURE. *It should remain until further notice.*

GEORGE *and* HARRY *dance to a song – another new song, or perhaps the same as in Act One – by David Bowie. Again, it builds on what we have already seen. It should feel like the culmination of something. It should inspire joy.*

*

A new caption appears: THE PAST. *It should remain until further notice.*

G. Fuck!

H. Came the cry from the living room, the following morning

G. Oh fuck

H. I'm halfway downstairs, when I see George slumped against the tank

G. It's Frances
She's laid

H. Laid?

G. Eggs
She's laid her eggs

H. Frances, too, was sort of slumped
The entire underside of her preferred rock was completely coated in clumps of tiny, translucent, grape-like orbs
Like some sort of miniature, ghost vineyard
She was entranced

Beat.

Does this mean you're going to be a grandmother, George?

G. Don't
It's not funny

H. You're a little on the young side, it has to be said, but it's hardly the end of the world

G. That's a matter of perspective, Harry
That depends entirely on whose world you're talking about

Beat.

Giving birth is the most important moment in a female octopus's life
They only do it once and so they have to get it right
They quite literally put all their eggs in one basket and they remain singularly focused on protecting their brood right up until the moment they hatch

H. But those eggs were never fertilised?

G. No

H. So that's never going to happen

G. Yes, well
Try telling her that

Beat.

The issue
Is that she's doing it anyway
She's behaving as if each of those eggs has a miniature, grain-sized Frances inside it

H. Even though she knows they don't?

G. What she 'knows' is unclear
Her body is awash with a powerful new hormonal cocktail that completely limits her psychological horizons to the underside of that rock

HARRY *thinks, hard.*

H. But that's… *fantastic*

G. No, it isn't

H. It's exactly the kind of genetically encoded irrationality that
I'm looking for
It's the chemically mandated victory of hope over experience
It's *faith*. George
Genetically pre-determined faith

G. *You don't understand*

H. It's a triumph!

G. Yeah, alright Harry, perhaps
But, it's also the end of the fucking road!

Beat.

Brooding octopuses guard their eggs and that's it
They don't hunt, or explore or *play*
Often, they don't even eat

Beat.

They don't *eat,* Harry
They *brood* and that's it
Until their eggs have hatched

H. So...

G. So, considering how *unlikely* that scenario is, there is every
chance that Frances will starve herself to death in the attempt

Beat.

And then I will lose everything
My best friend
My home
And the last vestiges of the life I shared with the man I loved
All gone

Beat.

And then, of course
There's you

Beat.

You won't stay, will you?

Pause.

H. Stay where?

G. No, of course not

H. You said it yourself. The university will kick you out of this
house, so stay where?
Why?

G. *Why?*
You're asking me why?

H. *George*, I won't have a paper to write
I won't have a job or anywhere to live

G. You'd have me
Harry
You would have me

Pause.

H. I...
I don't know what that means

*

H. She said, 'You've lost me completely'
And I said, 'It's very simple, Marianne'
'I just don't think I know how to give myself to another
person in the way that you want'
And she said 'No, no, I know that. That's what *I'm* saying'
'That's what *I'm* telling *you*'
'*You've* lost *me* completely'
'You've lost me, comma, completely'
And then she went

Beat.

When I realised that I wasn't scared of being alone, that was
it
I was free

Beat.

To be an anthropologist is to be a stranger to the world
It is to be

An imposter
It is to go out into the rarest, most far flung otherness you can
conceive of
Make a home there
And then, at some point, just... leave
And do it all over again, somewhere else
You can't do that if you can't be alone

Beat.

G. And with that, he drained the last dregs from his glass of
white wine and went back into the kitchen for another bottle

Beat.

This anecdote emerged the previous evening, by the way
The evening of the meal
After the cod's cheeks and the razor clams and the charm
offensive but before things...
Shifted

Beat.

Perhaps it didn't seem significant at the time or perhaps I
simply chose to forget it
But I think it deserves to be seen, now
So as to help make some sense of what follows

*

*The sound of some new Bowie song starts up, as if coming
from a specific location in the room. It is quiet at first, getting
louder until it is offensive. Then it cuts out to silence.*

GEORGE *and* HARRY*, however, play their dialogue to each
other as though the music can still be heard.*

H. George... this music...
She was drunk
She'd been drunk for days

G. Isn't it fantastic!?
I found a load of John's old records when I was clearing out
the office

H. *The office?*

G. Yeah!

H. George, I'd *really appreciate* you not going into the office
without my being there

G. What?

He talks louder, more deliberately.

H. I've quite a lot of papers containing sensitive information
All quite carefully arranged

G. Oh, I'm not interested in your stuff

H. Yes, I'm sure

G; I've been thinking, Harry
I've been thinking harder and faster than I have in months

H. Yes
Would you mind turning the music down, a little?

G. What?

H. Would you mind turning the music down!?

G. I can't hear you
I'll have to turn the music down

H. Thank you!

Beat. HARRY *sighs and relaxes, it's over. They speak, now,
at a normal volume.*

Thank you

G. She doesn't have a brain, did you know that?
Not *one* brain at least
Not one identifiable *seat* of consciousness
Rather, each of her eight legs is suffused with thought
And instinct
And perception and memory
In most animals some actions are *embodied* whereas others
stem from *the brain*
But what meaning do these definitions have for a creature,
like Frances, whose brain *is* her body?

Could it not almost be said, Harry…
Could it not be said that, in a way, what you're looking at,
when you look at Frances is not a body *or* a brain
Could it not be said that what you are looking at… is a kind
of… soul?

Beat. There are tears in GEORGE's *eyes.*

H. *George*

G. It's like she is moving into a different realm, Harry
Onto a higher plane
Think about that
Think about the… the… *ontological implications* of that for
a second
Don't you see?
Just because she won't eat on cue any more, that doesn't
meant that there isn't still *so much* to do

H. I'm going to go to bed, I think

G. No
Don't

H. Please keep the music down

G. No, no, no
I just need to play you something you'll know
Something you'll like
Hang on

H. *George*

G. One song, Harry
Just one

Beat.

H. Alright

G. That's the spirit

*It is 'Let's Dance' from Bowie's legendary Glastonbury set.
We hear it too.*

H. I don't know this, George

G. You will
   You will

   *We hear the sound of crowds and then his voice, introducing
   the band.*

   You'll see
   Just wait

   HARRY *listens. He clocks what he's hearing.*

H. Ah
   Yes
   Alright
   Good choice

G. Thank you

   GEORGE *starts to dance. She should seem liberated, as if
   her brain and her body are one.*

   *The chorus hits in and both dance together now. Whereas
   before they have danced like competent but hesitant novices,
   here they dance with surpassing intensity and rehearsed
   virtuosity.*

   *The song stops. They stop. They are out of breath and full of
   joy.*

   I've been watching you

H. Oh yes?

G. I have been watching you for a while
   I, like you, am a professional watcher

H. ....Right
   Yes

G. I have been watching you and you have been watching me,
   and I imagine we've both come to pretty firm conclusions
   about what is going on here

H. Yes. Perhaps

G. Well
   I have to tell you, Harry

That
It is my firm feeling and my *professional opinion*
That you are, most likely, falling in love with me

Beat.

H. I don't think now is really...

G. Now, of course, you will no doubt insist that, rather, it is I
who am falling in love with you

H. Perhaps, yes

G. And that might well be the case, Harry
I would defer to your professional judgement on that
But I think it could be worth considering the possibility that I
might also have a point?
For your own sake as much as mine

H. I can't do this
I can't do this now

G. Yes but you have to
Because soon it will be too late

H. I'm going to bed. Goodnight

G. Before you know it, Harry
Before either of us know it
It will all be far too little, and far too late

Beat.

H. And she was right
It was

*

G. A soot-like smog enveloped the whole world
Billowing clouds of forbidding black as far as the eye could
see

Beat.

And no, this isn't a description of my hangover
This is Frances's tank, the morning after the night before
A great, inky cube

A great black block in the middle of my living room and
her weightless, wraithlike figure hanging, listless, in the
translucent liquid
Quite dead

Beat.

The filtration system for the tank had been ripped away
Something that she was supposed to be incapable of doing,
but I'm not surprised
Her natural curiosity and her sense of mischief got the better
of her, and in this case it was fatal

Beat.

Octopuses are very sensitive to changes in their environment
The PH balance in the water would have shifted quickly and
Frances likely panicked
A physical, animal impulse kicking in
She would've fired a jet of her ink as a kneejerk, defensive
manoeuvre and then, when that didn't make things better, she
would've inked again

Beat.

Octopus ink contains a cocktail of chemicals that are, in high
doses, quite fatal
And so with every new injection of toxins into the closed
world of the tank, another threat would be perceived and
another jet provided
Creating a cycle of ever-increasing injuriousness that led her
body, in the end, to simply shut down

Beat. She thinks.

The question of the filter remains, of course
Why, when she was ostensibly besotted with her unfertilised
brood, would she emerge from her lair to tamper with a
previously uninteresting piece of equipment?

Beat.

But then maybe the answer to that question is obvious
Maybe Frances saw which way the wind was blowing and
resolved to duck out early

Or maybe there was something else going on, entirely
Some new impulse towards martyrdom, perhaps
Something which sat beyond the bounds of human reason,
perception and sense

*

H. She was reading from a stack of loose papers
You're up early

G. Yes
Since dawn

Beat.

H. George, I asked you not to come in here without my
permission
We agreed that it would be *my* office

GEORGE *smirks or sneers or laughs, mockingly.*

G. 'Your' office

H. It is mine, George

G. No
It isn't

H. George, we agreed

G. Yes we agreed that it could be your office for as long as you
were living here, but you're not living here any more so it's
not your office
So there

Beat.

H. Everything had been returned, with photographic precision,
to the exact location it had occupied before my arrival
What have you done with my things?

G. They're packed
Downstairs
Ready to go

H. George, *what the fuck?*

G. You've made it quite clear that there is nothing here for you
other than your research, and so I thought I would spare you
the agony of a protracted goodbye and let you get on your
way

H. I said I would stay as long as there was a chance that Frances
might recover

GEORGE *laughs mockingly, again.*

G. Right
Yes
Of course

H. *At least* until then, George
And, after that... well, who knows, really... there is so much
still to think about

G. No, there isn't
Frances died in the night

Beat.

H. What?

G. Time's up, I'm afraid

Beat.

H. George, will you please stop reading for a moment and look
at me?

G. Almost finished

Pause.

H. George!

G. There

Beat.

Well?
Is there something you wanted to say?

H. I'm
...Sorry

Beat.

G. You're sorry

H. Yes

G. That's it, is it?

H. Yes

G. Right
Well
Don't be
She's done us a favour. She's ripped off the plaster
Tea? Coffee, before you go?
Come on, let's head down
I'll go and put these papers with the rest of your things

H. Excuse me?

G. Ripping read, Harry
Honestly, bravo
Can't say I understood all of it or, indeed, most of it, but I got
the gist
And boy
What a gist it is

H. I asked you not to go through my things

G. I didn't go through them. I was packing them away

H. I think it's probably the same difference when you end up
rifling through my private papers

G. Private papers?

H. Yes

G. This doesn't look like a private paper to me, Harry
This looks set for publication

H. It was a thought experiment

G. That's an interesting way of putting it

H. *George*

G. How many mere 'thought experiments' come replete with
half a dozen pages of citations and references?
How many 'thought experiments' get proffered up for peer
review?
How many 'thought experiments' have self-aggrandising
titles like 'Grief, Loneliness and the Octopus Totem: Studies
in Anthro-Cephalopod Co-Dependency'?

H. George…

G. Or journalistic, aphoristic, *prick-teasing* subtitles like 'The
Strange Case of the Great Professor Grey and Her Eight-
legged Emotional Support Animal'?

H. I wrote that when I first arrived
When I was frustrated and when I was angry

G. You weren't angry, Harry
I'm angry
This is what *angry* looks like
You, on the other hand, wrote this in cold blood!

H. George

G. I have never read anything so cynical
So snide
So *superior*

H. Please stop

G. So cool
So collected
So absolutely *Olympian* in its high-handedness!
What kind of 'rage', for example, would induce you into
writing this?

H. Please don't

G. 'In treating Frances in the ways I delineate here, it could be
deduced that
Rather than attempting to "enculturate" Frances as is her
stated aim
Professor Grey
Is

In fact
Seeking to make Frances "stand in for" or "represent" the
social group of which she
After the traumatic death of her husband
Is the sole surviving member
In other words
It could be argued that she has made Frances into the live-in
totem
For her Cultural Unit of One'

Beat.

H. You'd made it quite clear to me when I arrived that it was
you and Frances against the world

G. Oh, and I suppose you found that somewhat wounding, did
you?
Is that it?

H. Yes
I did, yes

G. Why?

H. Why?

G. Why was that *so hard* for you, when it's *so very clear* that
you don't even like me!?

H. I *do* like you

G. No

H. I always liked you

G. No, you don't
You love me

H. Oh for goodness' sake

G. You're *in love* with me
You're infatuated with me, but you don't *like* me
You don't even know me
You don't know me and you don't care if I get hurt

H. That is not true

Beat.

G. 'Generally speaking...'

H. I was never going to publish it!

G. '*Generally speaking,* totems serve to demarcate distinctions
and underwrite hierarchies *within* a group
In contrast, the internal logic of Grey's "Octo-cult" works
somewhat differently
For her, instead, Frances is the means by which the grieving
professor recuses herself from all meaningful social
taxonomies to which she'd previously belonged

Beat.

Friends and family and faculty members
Biologists, specifically, and academics, generally
The educated middle-classes
The English
Women
And even, in the end, humanity as whole
None of these social alignments remain meaningful to Grey
now as, instead, she associates herself *exclusively* with
Frances, her octopus chattel

Beat.

Moreover...'

H. *Jesus*

G. 'Whereas, in most such cases these "totemic oppositions" are
extrapolated from rudimentary *cosmetic* differences
The dichotomies identified and utilised by the professor
in the pursuit of her comprehensive social self-exclusion
could be described, more accurately, as "oppositions of
temperament"
For example'

H. George!

G. 'Whereas people are kind, octopuses are aggressive
Whereas people are trusting, octopuses are suspicious
Whereas people are friendly, octopuses are hostile
And

Thusly
So is Professor Grey'

Beat.

'Regardless of whether or not Grey has successfully taught
Frances to believe in God
It would seem that she has made a god of Frances
A god from whom she derives all the moral authority she
needs in order to legitimise her anti-social, alienating
behaviour
And so as to validate her
Small
Sad
Lonely life'

Pause.

H. I should've added to that list, George

Beat.

I should have added that whereas people are oblivious,
octopuses are attentive
Whereas people are stupid, octopuses are clever
Whereas people are ignorant, octopuses are curious
Whereas people are boring, octopuses are anything but
Whereas people are like people... octopuses are like nobody
I have ever met

Beat.

G. That's cute, Harry
But you're still just talking to me about Frances

Beat.

She isn't *my* emotional crutch, Harry
She isn't *my* totem pole to lean on
She's yours
And now she's dead
So where does that leave us?

*

H. The tank is gone

G. I had no further use for it

H. I didn't think you'd still be living here

G. The Director of Studies was surprisingly sympathetic
She's let me stay until the end of the academic year

H. Yes but still, after everything

G. Oh come on, Harry
You appreciate better than anyone my outsized emotional
attachment to this place
Or at least you've claimed to

H. I'm not here to fight

G. Okay, fine
So why are you here?

H. I just… never had the chance to really express how sorry I
was
About Frances

G. Still ventriloquising your feelings through the fucking
octopus then?

H. *George*

G. Don't be sorry
Most cephalopods only live for a brief, solitary year or two
Frances was incredibly lucky to have made it as far as she
did

H. Right, and what if it's not just a solitary life, George, what if
it's a lonely one too?

G. Should I appreciate the distinction?

H. It might be telling that you don't
Loneliness is a killer
Lonely people die young

G. So?

H. So, what if the thing keeping Frances alive was company?
What if the thing keeping Frances alive was you?

Beat.

G. Right
Yes

H. What if the thing keeping you alive was Frances?

G. Alright
Enough

H. Alright

G. Stay in your lane

H. I care about you, George. That's all

G. Really?

H. Yes

G. That's nice

Beat.

Still published the article though, didn't you?

H. A version of it, yes

Beat.

Since there was only one person on this planet whose
feelings might have been spared by my not doing so
And since said person had already broken into my office
Rifled through my private belongings
Read said article
And then kicked me out of both her house and her life

G. Alright

H. There didn't seem to be much reason not to
Especially since it was pretty much all I had to show for my
time here

G. Fine

H. And anyway, I was angry

G. I don't see why I should be punished for your emotional
incontinence, Harry

He explodes, momentarily.

H. Yeah well that's pretty fucking rich coming from you!

Beat.

G. Well, it seems to have caused something of the requisite
sensation so congratulations

H. That isn't fair

G. Speaking engagements are flooding in, I'm sure
Job offers
Book deals

H. How do you know about the book?

G. *Jesus*

H. Who told you?

G. I was joking, Harry
For fuck's sake

H. Right

G. Time for you to go, I think

H. I'm not going to do it

Beat.

I'm not going to write it
I've been offered a fellowship. I'm going to take that instead

Beat.

There's an island in French Polynesia
In ancient times, the fishing communities who lived there
worshipped the octopus as a God
Having become a French colony, the islanders converted to
Catholicism and, as such, they've since built a church on the
site of the ancient temple

But the funny thing is
Is that it still has eight sides

Beat.

G. Right

H. So, I'm going to go there
To see if I can find any latent, residual presence of their
former faith
It seemed, after all, like an apposite synthesis between my
PhD and....
Well
Whatever the fuck I thought I was doing here

G. Yes
That does sound rather perfect
Congratulations

H. It isn't perfect
It's far from perfect
It won't be perfect unless you come too

Beat. She laughs a little.

G. Under what auspices, Harry?
For what reason?

H. I thought we could do it together
The research I mean

G. That...
...Doesn't really sound like my wheelhouse

H. Of course it is

G. Let me show you out

H. I spend my life watching people, George

Beat.

Watching them and looking for... *sameness*
Trying to identify concepts and behaviours that persist
between people and across communities because that
sameness is the essence of culture, George

Culture is just another word for mindless conformity and that
is so
Depressing

Beat.

Again and again, all I see is the unthinking adoption of
socially pre-ascribed impulses
Again and again, the same message rings out
'This is all we are'
'This is all we are capable of being'
And then someone like you comes along
Who I cannot read
Who I cannot anticipate
Someone
To whom I can only *attend*
And what is remarkable, George
What is all the more remarkable, still
Is that you don't even see how truly extraordinary that makes
you

G. I see it perfectly well
You're the one who struggled

H. Never
Not with that
Not with the…
Doing of it
Not with the *being*…
In…
Of it
I just
Don't have the words, is all

Pause.

G. I think it's all just been a·bit too much, actually
I think it's all just been a bit too hard and a bit too sad and I
think I just associate you far too heavily with a very unhappy
time in my life
So thank you
For thinking of me

But it is too late
It's too late, and it is a 'no', but thank you

Silence.

H. She didn't say any of that, of course

G. No
That would, in itself, have been far too much for this strange, failed moment to bear

H. So
Instead…

G. Instead I went over to the record player and I played a sad song

H. Not David Bowie this time, but rather something 'of the moment'

G. Yes, it was something new
Something
Which spoke to now

The caption which reads THE PAST *fades, and is replaced with one that reads;* NOW.

A sad song plays. They slow dance. GEORGE *takes* HARRY*'s face in her hands. She looks like she might kiss him, but she doesn't. She whispers in his ear something that the audience should absolutely not be able to hear. She whispers:*
'To have been in your thoughts
Is to have stood in the sun'

And then she leaves the stage for the first time and HARRY *is left alone.*

End of play.

www.nickhernbooks.co.uk

facebook.com/nickhernbooks

twitter.com/nickhernbooks